# 日期

Early Literacy Series : Level A

Copyright © 2022 by Level Learning, INC.

All rights reserved. No part of this book may be reproduced in any form or by any electronic or mechanical means without permission in writing from the publisher.

ISBN 978-1-64040-137-2

Content by Jingyao Qi
Illustration by Matt Austin

Published by Level Learning, INC.

**About Level Learning:**

Level Learning provides a Chinese literacy focused curriculum for K-12 classrooms. Our data driven literacy system allows teachers to better understand and more accurately assess the development of student's literacy. Our program includes 40 levels of Language Skills, Reading Skills and Book Leveling for fiction and non-fiction, as well as formative online assessments and data analytics to inform instruction.

To learn more about our entire offering, visit **www.levellearning.com**

**About Level Learning Early Literacy Offering:**

Level Learning Early Literacy offering provides a structured and systematic approach to teaching the most commonly used Chinese characters to new learners. Our offering teaches characters through story-telling and themes that are familiar to young learners.

Level Learning provides two unique Early Literacy offering – 1) book series and 2) assessment and tracking system.

Book Series include:
- 12 leveled books across levels A through D
- Games for students to practice what they've learned
- Teachers' guide with stories and key teaching points to help teach characters in the context of a story

To download games and teacher's guide, visit **www.levellearning.com**

Assessment and Tracking system is available as part of Level Learning subscription and provides mastery-based online assessment and data analytics for every level to show student's learning progress and gap. To start a subscription, contact **support@levellearning.com**.

日

月

星

日

大

日

星期一　星期二　星期三　星

 → 星

日

昨天 今

天　明天

人

→ 明

# 月

2 0

| 一月 | | | | | | |
|---|---|---|---|---|---|---|
| 日 | 一 | 二 | 三 | 四 | 五 | 六 |
|  | 1 | 2 | 3 | 4 | 5 | 6 |
| 7 | 8 | 9 | 10 | 11 | 12 | 13 |
| 14 | 15 | 16 | 17 | 18 | 19 | 20 |
| 21 | 22 | 23 | 24 | 25 | 26 | 27 |
| 28 | 29 | 30 | 31 | | | |

| 二月 | | | | | | |
|---|---|---|---|---|---|---|
| 日 | 一 | 二 | 三 | 四 | 五 | 六 |
| | | | | 1 | 2 | 3 |
| 4 | 5 | 6 | 7 | 8 | 9 | 10 |
| 11 | 12 | 13 | 14 | 15 | 16 | 17 |
| 18 | 19 | 20 | 21 | 22 | 23 | 24 |
| 25 | 26 | 27 | 28 | | | |

| 五月 | | | | | | |
|---|---|---|---|---|---|---|
| 日 | 一 | 二 | 三 | 四 | 五 | 六 |
| | | 1 | 2 | 3 | 4 | 5 |
| 6 | 7 | 8 | 9 | 10 | 11 | 12 |
| 13 | 14 | 15 | 16 | 17 | 18 | 19 |
| 20 | 21 | 22 | 23 | 24 | 25 | 26 |
| 27 | 28 | 29 | 30 | 31 | | |

| 六月 | | | | | | |
|---|---|---|---|---|---|---|
| 日 | 一 | 二 | 三 | 四 | 五 | 六 |
| | | | | | 1 | 2 |
| 3 | 4 | 5 | 6 | 7 | 8 | 9 |
| 10 | 11 | 12 | 13 | 14 | 15 | 16 |
| 17 | 18 | 19 | 20 | 21 | 22 | 23 |
| 24 | 25 | 26 | 27 | 28 | 29 | 30 |

| 九月 | | | | | | |
|---|---|---|---|---|---|---|
| 日 | 一 | 二 | 三 | 四 | 五 | 六 |
| | | | | | | 1 |
| 2 | 3 | 4 | 5 | 6 | 7 | 8 |
| 9 | 10 | 11 | 12 | 13 | 14 | 15 |
| 16 | 17 | 18 | 19 | 20 | 21 | 22 |
| 23 | 24 | 25 | 26 | 27 | 28 | 29 |
| 30 | | | | | | |

| 十月 | | | | | | |
|---|---|---|---|---|---|---|
| 日 | 一 | 二 | 三 | 四 | 五 | 六 |
| | 1 | 2 | 3 | 4 | 5 | 6 |
| 7 | 8 | 9 | 10 | 11 | 12 | 13 |
| 14 | 15 | 16 | 17 | 18 | 19 | 20 |
| 21 | 22 | 23 | 24 | 25 | 26 | 27 |
| 28 | 29 | 30 | 31 | | | |

## 三月

| 日 | 一 | 二 | 三 | 四 | 五 | 六 |
|---|---|---|---|---|---|---|
|  |  |  |  | 1 | 2 | 3 |
| 4 | 5 | 6 | 7 | 8 | 9 | 10 |
| 11 | 12 | 13 | 14 | 15 | 16 | 17 |
| 18 | 19 | 20 | 21 | 22 | 23 | 24 |
| 25 | 26 | 27 | 28 | 29 | 30 | 31 |

## 四月

| 日 | 一 | 二 | 三 | 四 | 五 | 六 |
|---|---|---|---|---|---|---|
| 1 | 2 | 3 | 4 | 5 | 6 | 7 |
| 8 | 9 | 10 | 11 | 12 | 13 | 14 |
| 15 | 16 | 17 | 18 | 19 | 20 | 21 |
| 22 | 23 | 24 | 25 | 26 | 27 | 28 |
| 29 | 30 |  |  |  |  |  |

## 七月

| 日 | 一 | 二 | 三 | 四 | 五 | 六 |
|---|---|---|---|---|---|---|
| 1 | 2 | 3 | 4 | 5 | 6 | 7 |
| 8 | 9 | 10 | 11 | 12 | 13 | 14 |
| 15 | 16 | 17 | 18 | 19 | 20 | 21 |
| 22 | 23 | 24 | 25 | 26 | 27 | 28 |
| 29 | 30 | 31 |  |  |  |  |

## 八月

| 日 | 一 | 二 | 三 | 四 | 五 | 六 |
|---|---|---|---|---|---|---|
|  |  |  | 1 | 2 | 3 | 4 |
| 5 | 6 | 7 | 8 | 9 | 10 | 11 |
| 12 | 13 | 14 | 15 | 16 | 17 | 18 |
| 19 | 20 | 21 | 22 | 23 | 24 | 25 |
| 26 | 27 | 28 | 29 | 30 | 31 |  |

## 十一月

| 日 | 一 | 二 | 三 | 四 | 五 | 六 |
|---|---|---|---|---|---|---|
|  |  |  |  | 1 | 2 | 3 |
| 4 | 5 | 6 | 7 | 8 | 9 | 10 |
| 11 | 12 | 13 | 14 | 15 | 16 | 17 |
| 18 | 19 | 20 | 21 | 22 | 23 | 24 |
| 25 | 26 | 27 | 28 | 29 | 30 |  |

## 十二月

| 日 | 一 | 二 | 三 | 四 | 五 | 六 |
|---|---|---|---|---|---|---|
|  |  |  |  |  |  | 1 |
| 2 | 3 | 4 | 5 | 6 | 7 | 8 |
| 9 | 10 | 11 | 12 | 13 | 14 | 15 |
| 16 | 17 | 18 | 19 | 20 | 21 | 22 |
| 23 | 24 | 25 | 26 | 27 | 28 | 29 |
| 30 | 31 |  |  |  |  |  |

www.ingramcontent.com/pod-product-compliance
Lightning Source LLC
Chambersburg PA
CBHW040326100526
44584CB00002BA/264